# Doggerel
## and other doggerel

poems by George J. Dance

Principled Press
Toronto, Ontario, Canada

Lulu Press
Baltimore, MD, USA

**2015**

*Doggerel, and other doggerel: poems* by George J. Dance

Published by Lulu Press for Principled Press.

ISBN 978-0-9948600-0-2

An earlier version of "7/16/69" was published in *Option* 2:6
(November-December, 1974). "I Am a Splash" and "Bus
Ride on a Summer Night" were first published in *Other
Voices International* 42 (2008).

First printing: September  2015
Printed in U.S.A.

2

# Doggerel
## and other doggerel

# Contents

# March

Snow becomes mud
becomes a mighty river
to the young boy

# I Am a Splash

I am a splash; the pond abides
Serenely after I am done.
Such different thoughts when I was young:
Back then, I thought I'd rule the wide
Ocean, and command its tide.
Yet still those rocks and stones I take
And cast them into every lake
And pond, and every brook and stream,
Inspired by a constant dream:
To see how big a splash I'll make.

# Spring Again

It's spring again, and I am with Maureen.
I'd add "thank God for that" (if I believed)
For frozen as in high beams I have seen
Oncoming dread: one dead and one bereaved.
No hope for us to live eternally
Or garner brave new bodies after death,
No more than this, the thought impelling me
To get untharn, to fight for every breath –
A battle till the setting of each sun,
A victory each sunset we survive,
Another day my love and I have won
And death has lost. Today we are alive,
   This world is ours, its grass and trees are green,
   It's spring again, and I am with Maureen.

# Round the Mercury

*time (that savaged emerald)*
*flows like scaffold spiders*
*or money without price.*
  *- "Mercury Switches & the Mating of Clocks," Alacrity Stone*

kissed by gold
is her lovely
skate backwards
round the mercury

from the first spark
brass candle holders
silver cherubs
bronze cylinders

He laughs, their steps
in unison
mirroring soles
of frozen men

their podium
the uterus
that wrinkled jewel
bequeathed to us

and Jesus like
a wingless blur
hums  the daffodils
over her

time flows like money
without price
steel blades scar
and cut the ice

vibration shuddering
the heart
into grace
and into art

# At the Palais

Ben and Bea met one night
At the Palais, in early spring.
They disagreed on everything.
It ended in a nasty fight:
A case of hatred at first sight.

The Palais is long derelict,
Their steps are slow, their hair is white,
But still they quarrel day and night
For Ben loves Bea (as you'd predict)
And Beatrice loves Benedict.

# Mars & Avril

Mars the Brat marched in with the melting snow,
blew around town, whistling at all the chicks
and trying to lift up every second skirt;
Mars, that crazy, schizophrenic Brat,
one minute waterbombing us for kicks,
next minute grabbing some poor sucker's hat
to fling it like a gauntlet in the dirt
while in his eyes a killing cold would show.

Then Avril flew in like a vernal breeze
and though the Brat dissed that girl's style of bling –
her flowers, rainbows, birds in blossomed trees –
she made him laugh, and cry, and even sing,
and slowly, gently as a meadow breathes,
the Brat went down, disarmed by love in spring.

# April

Sky a cold shower
Dousing bilious ground.
Still the kindest month.

# The poem at 3 a.m.

The poem at 3 a.m.
Does not want to be written;
It visits only to mock you.

# Masterpiece

He's worked on that one poem for seven years.
He's polished, tweaked, thrown whistles in and bells,
To make it Art (no, not the tripe that sells
In glossy magazines at which he sneers),
A modern masterpiece – and yet he fears
His time's been wasted, for it never gels.
Why must he suffer seven years of hells
To take his rightful place among the seers?

   If he could find the formula – wash, rinse,
Repeat  – he'd show his greatness then and there!
The critics all would bow, the rhymesters wince.
His brilliance, wit, good looks, and lovely hair
Could make him Laureate, or even Prince
Of Poetry, if only life were fair!

# Reply to a *Critico*

*Vaya caprichosa danza*
*la de este señor que rima*
*como colegial, y encima,...*
*ni perezoso ni corto,*
*sólo rima cada enésima.*
*:-)*
–    *OB, May 2007*

"Sólo rima cada enésima"?
Now, how am I to write an answer
when I can't read one line or stanza?
I think, I guess, this señor's tema
is:  I'm no poet, just a dreamer.
I'll state what I've already said:
I too could Pound out complex verse,
incomprehensible or worse,
but wish to write so I'll be read:
the unheard are already dead.

# postpoetry

although there's nothing left to say
we're gonna say it anyway
& if a reader doesn't read
we'll call him something we don't need
& if a critic calls it shit
we won't believe a word of it
& if a poet points that out
we'll just ignore it & we'll shout
about her frogs and trees and birds
so we won't have to read her words

or better yet let's write of war
and fill a page or two with gore
some reeking flesh a severed head
& maggots feasting on the dead
& if perchance that doesn't shock
let's add a line of fuck ass cock
motherfucker piss & shit
(who knows that just might pass for wit)

what else to do what else to say
when everything is mere cliche?
how else to make a reader feel
or think that what we say is real?
of course the whole idea is dumb
when we're as comfortably numb
but if we sweat through every motion
we may feel a real emotion –
well, it kills an hour or two
and we have nothing else to do

# Ponder This

Alas! Alack! Oh, woe is me!
I am in Mohit Misery.

I spent good money on a book
of poems without a preview look

then found, when I had ope'd it up
row after row of silly coup-

lets, half of which don't scan
(though the poet gets a rhyme in whenever he can)

while the other half make zero sense;
a carpark often has a fence.

In life there's many a tragedy,
but none like Mohit Misery.

I'll even pray to heaven, please
relieve us from Mo Miseries.

# The Song of the Smug Academic

You thought this was a usenet group, where anyone
    could play,
Where all could write and criticize – Well, that was
    yesterday,
For I have raised a mighty force of usenet kooks, and we
Have taken over. Welcome to PJ's Academy.

The first thing you must learn is: Follow my poetic rules.
I've many you would never learn in colleges or schools.
No one's allowed to break these rules – except, of
    course, for me;
I make 'em and I break 'em at PJ's Academy.

Rule #1, of course, is to proclaim me a true poet,
And all my friends as well (for if we don't, who'd ever
    know it?),
And all our poems wonderful. We're a society
Of mutual admiration at PJ's Academy.

The most important feature of a poem is whom it's by:
It's great if it's by one of us, or by some famous guy,
And otherwise it's trash. Apply that rule, and you'll be
    free
From having to learn anything at our Academy.

Harass all others posting here, to chase them all away.
Tell them their verses make no sense, their every word's
    cliche:
They don't know how to write, so they should give up

    poetry
And leave it to the experts of PJ's Academy.

But if you find a writer who will not do what we say,
Who reads and studies for himself, and writes another
        way,
Then drive him out of here at once, for he's the enemy
And we don't want his kind here at PJ's Academy;

So call him every name you can to get him out of here:
A plagiarist, a pedophile, a racist, and a queer.
Insult his work, his name, his looks, his job, his family.
Be liars for the higher truth of our Academy.

Then, if you follow all these rules, and do all we advise –
The flattery, discouragement, invective, smears, and
        lies –
We'll call you a real poet (though, alas!, there's no
        degree),
And even let you teach here at PJ's Academy.

# The Maestro

Not much is like a Hammy Hogarth sonnet,
So fluently and smoothly doth it ooze
The while it reeks of bigotry and booze –
A heap of feces with sweet perfume on it? –
A ghoulish monster in an Easter bonnet? –
Thus illustrating either lack of clues
Or lack of thought; for Hammy did not choose,
With any line, to waste much time upon it:

    Twelve minutes max was all that he would spend
On fourteen lines; in that way he could crank
Out many copies of the same old sonnet,
Each one of which would please his any friend,
If not the Muse herself – but not the bank,
For Hammy could not sell or even pawn it.

# Minor Incident

Those Berkshire bookshops had no stairs that wind,
But once we climbed a different sort of stair
In search of poetry – only to find
A bald, decrepit crone declaiming there.
It danced and pranced and flounced across the stage,
It ranted and it raved of "poet's day,"
It shrieked of killer dwarfs; and in its rage,
It drenched the first five rows in spittle-spray.

You pointed, out the window, at the dock
To where a mongrel lay upon some waste
In ratty splendour, licking at its cock,
Oblivious to all but its own taste.
    No poetry in that room, just a bore,
    But you, dear, found a perfect metaphor.

# May

How like a tree
to strew its blossoms
on my flowerbed!

# Spring Scene

In broken land the hills remain
And grass and trees are lush again.
My teardrops fall upon new flowers –
Birds flit – I pace and mourn the hours,
The flames of war now three months old,
A word from home more dear than gold.
I scratch my head; white hair too thin
To even hold a hairpin in.

*by Tu Fu*
*translated by George J. Dance*

# Only the Lonely

The man in shades
strides to the mic
and declares,
"Only the lonely
know the way I feel tonight . . ."
– and ten thousand screaming,
chanting fans wedged up against
each other in the hall all together
suddenly feel so
lonely.

# Boots

Two boots, the same
down to the very laces,
kicking each other.

# Doggerel

The rowdy dogs that frolic in the park
may run, and jump, and gambol gracefully,
but all dogs, when they spy a likely tree,
must lift a nether leg and leave a mark.
Some dogs must growl at every bird and frog,
and some must leave their stools upon the street,
and some must bark at every other dog,
and some must snap at every poor man's feet.
A man who's being dogged must learn to fight,
to put the boots to any mangy cur
that's troubled by the fleas amidst its fur
and make the mongrel yowl! Then doggie might
    run off to find a more defenceless bone
    and leave the weary traveller alone.

# Pizzanashad

What is the good of ordering a pizza
when every slice has several hundred calories
(that's not to mention any oily trans fats,
plus tons and more tons of cholesterol)?

What is the good of ordering a pizza
when nowadays it's just so darned expensive
(last night I had to fork out $30
for six small slices and ten bony wings)?

What is the good of ordering a pizza
when next you have to wait for 40 minutes
(unless, like half the time, the driver ends up
lost, and then the pizza ends up cold)?

What is the good of ordering a pizza?
Deliver me a salad and a drink.

# Country Wife

Our dog died, and then you lost the baby,
Then John went blind, and Grandma took her life,
But you stood by my side without a maybe,
Forever loving me, my country wife.

I drank, I cheated, and you cried you missed me.
The crops failed and the floods came every year.
But when they took the house and truck you kissed me
Then took my hand and walked with me to here.

If you had not've loved me, dear, and stayed, it
Would be the death of me, all of this strife.
It's only thanks to you that I have made it,
Forever by my side, my country wife.

A country man may live a troubled life,
But, Lord, it's worth it with a country wife.

# This is Just too Gay

all the plums?
you bitch

no I won't
forgive you

you're getting
such a slap

# Homophobia?

Gay people have rights, I'll admit;
Some have charm, some have grace, some have wit.
    I never will go
      To a gay picnic, though:
The hot dogs must all taste like shit.

# Religions

*A Martian poem*

The Hindu takes a sacred vow,
And never, ever eats a cow.

The Muslim thinks a cow's too big,
And so he never eats a pig.

The Jew does like the Muslim, though
You mustn't ever tell them so.

Wafers'n'wine for Christian God,
Except on Fridays, when it's cod.

Religions are the same, I guess:
First you sin, and then confess

And then a holy man will bless,
Dressed up in a fancy dress.

# the workers do not dream

the workers do not dream
of renouncing love
inexplicably
they cling to this
final bastion of exploitation
while the dogs piss
on their legs & dry-hump
their empty dreams
& the fat cats whip
them in bondage
while their severed hands
make good paperweights
for upper management
even as their disillusionment
is torn from them
as the dog
tears flesh from the bone
still they cling
to that one part
to that sweet dream
their eulogy
as if perpetually
anchored


*lines by  aapc collective*
*poem by George J. Dance*


26

# Hollywood Slut

They called the woman strumpet, harlot, slut:
Words of nuts designed to stab and cut,
Toilet language snippets spread like smut,
No chance to find out what or to rebut.

They called the woman slut, harlot, strumpet,
Blasted from the pulpits like a trumpet:
From every jealous Dick and peeping Tom, it
Gushed, the prophet-zealot-preacher vomit.

They called the woman strumpet, slut, harlot,
Branding her with words of flaming scarlet
(Never respite for the hand-made varlet):
Burn her on a faggot! – Make her Starlet!

They called the woman harlot, strumpet, slut,
Then left her but a tithe of their own cut.

*by Dennis M. Hammes & George J. Dance*

# June

Bright flowers crawl
from torn silk,
dry and blow away

# Riverview

I will take you down
to where the waters meet,
to the river running majestic
through dark cathedral aisles
seeking the salt gift
at the wide & watery altar.
        You will say,
"What a marvellous view.
How just like the postcard, too."

# Poet in a Porsche

Why do you drive through the woods in cars,
Faking so much and so much?
Go home and write about malls and bars;
Why do you drive through the woods in cars?
The light on the leaves like a million stars
You will never see, for you're out of touch.
Why do you drive through the woods in cars,
Faking so much and so much?

# In the Garden

First rose of spring
blooms in the garden,
where my lady lingers.

# Bird Song

*I do not thrive; I only speak,*
*so softly, about whining things.*
*In my mind, the dead bird sings*
*and all things lost pass from its beak.*
                    *—   Karen Tellefson, 2007*


"And all things lost pass from its beak"
in song (I hope; if real a mess
would be on table, floor, and dress,
to clean up which might take a week) —
a friendly tune when one feels weak.

Though to that song mine can't compare,
a singing bird in bush or air
is worth three dead ones in the mind.
Let's take a walk outside to find
the joy of birdsong, everywhere

30

# Elixir (Dance Mix)

Life is but a dance through time
when laughing music fills the air
and sweet melody your mind.

What is greater than the beat
of the drum? – this heartfelt rhythm,
leading partner of desire.

Fret not, if your feet falter,
you can always find the rhythm:
Listen for the melody,
let your heart echo the beat.
Find the hidden harmony.

Touch the notes moving, gliding,
let them sing this time inside you.
Hear them, they are all you have.
Taste them, for they are sublime.
Know them, for they will endure.

*by Crystal Matteau & George J. Dance*

# If beauty were light

If beauty were light
which it isn't
the dawn would be
incandescent
while you
would be neon.

# My Lady and the Dawn

My Lady is not fairer than the Dawn
But still I swear I hold her far more dear,
For I'm abed, and Daybreak comes anon –
Its pleasures yet to taste – while she is here.

# Romance Novel

## I

You're never serious at 17.
One great night, full of pints and lemonade,
You've had enough of cafés, so you stroll
Beneath green lime trees on the promenade.

The lime trees smell so good at night in June!
Sometimes the air's so soft you have to blink.
The wind from off the town is charged with noise
And smells of grape, of ale and stronger drink . . .

## II

Look there, you see a tiny handkerchief
Of dark blue, framed by branches in the night,
Pierced by a hapless star that melts away
With one soft shudder, beautifully white . . .

You're 17! In June! It gets you high –
The sap's champagne: it makes your whole head
     ring . . .
You ramble – suddenly you feel a kiss
That flutters on your lips like a live thing . . .

## III

Below the halo of a pale street lamp,
Your heart invents a novel, going mad
Because a young miss stopped to sneak a glance
Beneath the menacing shadow of her dad . . .


And just because she thinks you're such a child,
She trots on by and swings her little hips
And gives a shrug that slugs you in the gut,
While cavatinas die upon your lips . . .


## IV

Now you're in love – till August anyway.
You'll make her laugh! You'll write her poetry!
But still you're shunned as if you tasted bad
Until, one night, the dear one writes to thee!


That night you wander back to the cafés.
You order up more pints and lemonade . . .
You're never serious at 17
When limes grow green above the promenade.


*by Arthur Rimbaud*
*translated by George J. Dance*

# Lucky Penny

Hey there, Lucky Penny,
    Shining like brand new.
Hey there, Lucky Penny,
    Can I get lucky with you?

I saw you in an alleyway
    Shining in the sun.
I knew it was my lucky day,
    You were my lucky one.
So many guys had passed you by
    And left you all alone,
But I knew I just had to try
To pick you up and bring you home.

Hey there, Lucky Penny.
    Oh, what I would do
For a Lucky Penny.
    Let me get lucky with you.

I'd wanted you from long before
    When I was just a lad.
I've had my share of luck and more
    But most of it was bad.
Each night before I'd go to sleep
    I'd dream about how grand
My life would be if I could keep
A Lucky Penny in my hand.

Hey there, Lucky Penny,
    Make my dreams come true.

Be my Lucky Penny.
    Let me get lucky with you.

My luck has changed from that day on;
    The good times have been many.
I don't care if my money's gone,
    I only need a Penny.
I never had a clue before
    That life could hold such thrills.
I wouldn't trade my Penny for
A billion brand-new dollar bills.

Hey there, Lucky Penny,
    Thanks are overdue.
You're my Lucky Penny.
    I got lucky with you.

# Let's Write a Poem

Let's write a poem,
a brittle old tune.
I saw you walking to Seaside Park
& so does your mom, too:
"Strumpet in lacy pantaloons
like a prostitute
playing her mark!"
She knows how
to make a commotion.
Bathtub waves upon the ocean.
Sunny afternoon
in the park,
you were a sonnet in bloom.

Let's drop a bomb,
a poem & a song;
I've been waiting here for hours.
Golden sunlight pierces Neptune
through soft swirls of blue
& the daylight is ours.
When the cement dries
there'll be no you nor I
driving through life,
turn signal on.
Stay out of the ruts of cliche.

Stay out of the dark.
Don't bark at the moon.
Watch your back in the park
with your bodyguard goon,

playing him higher & higher
like a serpent in the night
till he threw back his head
& howled!
His head the wolf must devour
with spackles of stars
in the shackles of hours,
for his is the night
& the daylight is ours,
the golden ray split
between carnage & flowers –
let's write a poem today.


*lines by aapc collective*
*poem by George J. Dance*

# July

Children gasp
as the sky comes alive
with friendly fire.

# Sensation

In the hot summer days of shimmering blue
I shall wander uncharted frontiers,
With the grasses prickling and cooling my soles
And the breezes bathing my ears.

Not a word shall I speak, not a thought shall I think
As I wander with nothing to guide me,
But my spirit shall fill with unlimited love,
As if for a woman beside me.

*by Arthur Rimbaud*
*translated by George J. Dance*

# Daysleepers

Somewhere a violated auto
shrieks a one-note alarm
in brilliant sunshine;
the poet rolls over,
wills himself to sleep.


The long-haired blonde
sprawled naked at his feet
is clearly winning
this sleep-competition,
tail and paws perfectly still.


atop the bookcase
a fat ball
of tri-coloured fur


warms up
for the next round

# Flowers for Vera

**1**

Vera, like Venus
in the viridescence,
picking vivid violets
with oblanceolate
leaves.

**2**

Vera vamps
at her vanity,
anticipating violins.
Violets still vivid
in a vase.

**3**

Venerable old Vera
flips frailly through
a volume of verse,
removes a pressed
and faded violet.

# 7/16/69

"Observe the land," one said,
"How small is man."
A railway.
"Observe the sea," one said,
"How small is man."
A steamship.
"Observe the sky," one said,
"How small is man."
An airplane.

How small is man?
He reaches for his height.

"Observe the heavens," one said,
"How small is man."
Apollo.

# Bus Ride on a Summer Night

Bus crammed, I squeeze and stumble to a seat,
Loathing the heat, rank sweat, and noise, so I
Avert my gaze, stare at a cobalt sky
And miles of matching boxes on the street

Which cut to a new picture suddenly –
Black velvet crossed by lines of red and white
Clear shining beads, bright rosaries of light
Stretching past the horizon towards infinity . . .

I see the threads that run through every bead,
Each prayer and fear, each joy and agony,
Entangling into one humanity:
One flesh, one blood, from one uncommon seed –

It's passed; I shift, relax into my seat,
And breathe in human life, so warm, so sweet.

# At the Gates of Dawn

Night prowls, scratches sand, & then pads on,
the gnomes are sleeping in their gnomish homes,
when darkness is increased by 1, to 7
& from the icy waters underground

a scarlet eagle rises, showering gold
on all.  Floating down, the light resounds
blindingly – flap flicker flicker / Blam pow pow –

& all the land is lime &  limpid green.
Amidst the grass, dandelions thrive.
Buttercups cup the light in the foggy dew.

Change, return, success, going & coming,
nothing can be destroyed once & for all:
Look at the sun, look at the sky, look at the river
lazily winding, finding its way to sea.

# Light of Day

The clouds of heaven roaming whitely by,
exotic beasts across a cyan sky –
black clouds stampeding on the ground – they rule
this sauna world; they dim but do not cool
     & as they pass it blows my mind:
     a silent symphony I find
     when shadows fold & drop away
     into the lemon light of day.

The trees are fountaining – cascades of green
declare their beauty for my dear Maureen;
the green is falling, flooding all the ground,
a verdant sea in which I long to drown
     & as it falls, I want to cry
     to know that all of this will die,
     that everything must wash away
     beneath the liquid light of day.

Her body fits me like a silken glove.
The sun is burning on my back with love.
Past life sustains anew life, layer on layer,
while brass of birdsong blows throughout the air
     & as it blows thoughts pass my mind:
     this light outside is hers & mine
     for it will always be this way,
     right here, right now where we will stay
     within the living light of day.

# August

sun-hardened earth
waits panting for the first crack
of thunder

# Fuji-san

Under the flaring sun,
Fuji-san wears his
White-straw *sugegasa*.

# The Frontier

I

The frontier begins
here, where we think:
heartland – the point
in universal space
where we all begin,
a moment discovered
within a man's life.
No trip ever ends
here in heartland;
to find the frontier
one must seek elsewhere –
perhaps the woods,
the shield, or beyond.
The frontier escapes
in all directions,
falls below the straight line,
like much
– becomes imaginary.

Image.
Sky.
Grasp.  Focus
for a lifetime of travel
for a man to
find himself within
too plentiful and higher
lifetimes of climbing. Man
is what the scale measures.
(Dissolve to self:)

Seeking yourself
in cavern-shrouded
myth   world   culture
cerebrum   and fingers
slowly creeping
you succeed.
Do you wonder
who completely understood?


II


the river is coursing
in its carved channel
tumultuous
stultifying stump-cluttered
power reaching
in distance toward
                    corpses
on burial poles
underneath a mackerel sky
same scene but now a graveyard
of weed-strewn mounds
a cluster of pronghorns
on the brow
towering high
clouds:  fenced
and unfortunate
sky intimating
could-be alive

when we talk

wherever
we talk
also about space
lost   gaunt   empty
things   and people
seasons of the miles
and straight lines cut
through cordillera
to fort
to ocean
to mountain
hope


## III


The ancient dreams
are dying, yielding
to silence.  I am
no more here than elsewhere;
for those who lived
the greater I fear
how frail it is now,
bound, imprisoned.
There is a killer,
smiling yet a killer.  Yet
to believe in the frontier
is utmost.  As we live,
selves turning
to islands
and beyond,
within many an unknown
hope and destiny
the frontier shall live.

# Vowels

Black A, white E, red I, green U, blue O: you vowels,
Some day I'll tell the tale of where your mystery lies:
Black A, a jacket formed of hairy, shiny flies
That buzz among harsh stinks in the abyss's bowels;

White E, the white of kings, of moon-washed fogs and
      tents,
Of fields of shivering chervil, glaciers' gleaming tips;
Red I, magenta, spat-up blood, the curl of lips
In laughter, hatred, or besotted penitence;

Green U, vibrating waves in viridescent seas
Or peaceful pastures flecked with beasts – furrows of
      peace
Imprinted on our brows as if by alchemies;

Blue O, great Trumpet blaring strange and piercing cries
Through Silences where Worlds and Angels pass
      crosswise;
Omega, O, the violet brilliance of Those Eyes!


*by Arthur Rimbaud*
*translated by George J. Dance*

# On Dover Beach

*Abstract: Arnold's speaker is a young soldier who wants a piece before he goes off to fight, and tries to get it by arousing his girl's sympathy.*

The above cynical tone
is not Matthew Arnold's, of course, but my own.
Hmm . . . seems from rhyming I can't resist,
but I digress . . . Arnold employs a protagonist,
a persona: A youth soon off to fight
(therefore armies clashing in the night)
– to fight against France, of course
(hence Dover, within sight of enemy shores),
not at all himself: Arnold's imagination
conceives a tragic figure,
man trapped in his station.

'The consciousness of the time' – aye, that's the clue:
The mind of Arnold's lover is not that of me nor you.
He is, so unlike us, a man with a set place
and knows it well, like all the educated of his race.
I see a lord's second son, and therefore born to serve
in army or in navy (active duty, not reserve)
seeing well his own demise one not-too-future morn;
how it must and would be
from the second he was born.

I'm quite convinced our speaker's only plan
is to grab what little pleasure that he can:
some food, some drink, for now a little fluff
knowing that is all he gets, not nearly enough

to change his fate one jot. He sees it clear
and tries to show that sadness to his dear:
that she's as trapped as he, both trapped that way,
with no more choice for tomorrow than yesterday
which, in his case, means marching to the folly
no freer than the ocean (note the latter's melancholy).

Can we understand, can we really feel
this sorrow without knowing why?
The onus is on us, of course. We have to try
to set aside our own worldview
for that which Arnold's lover and his lady knew,
of men like flies, caught in the web
of their destinies
as in the ancient Greek tragedies
(hence the allusion to Sophocles).

As flies we are to the gods; they kill us for their sport,
with "Eat, drink, love, be merry now" our sole retort;
      then, like the fly,
         after our meal,
           and our bit of love
all we can do is march off to die.

# Gardeners of Eden

*after Alistair Graham*


In Africa, gazelles roam the savannah
With various and sundry other beasts:
Hyenas, lions, zebras cross the plain.
You, too, can fly first-class to ogle nature
There in the raw, to see life live and die
In pristine habitat, unspoiled by man.

Adjust the focus, though, and there is man
In tiny huts that dot the wide savannah;
In starkest poverty they live and die
Half-starving, like the other native beasts:
An early death to keep the balance of nature,
Another pile of bones upon the plain.

One backward look's enough to make it plain
That such was once the lot of every man,
A brute existence at the grace of nature:
Starvation stalked in forest and savannah,
Diseases, dangers lurking both from beasts
And other men – they learned to kill or die.

Today we do much more than live and die
Like that. Look forward now: Is it not plain
We can be something more than merely beasts,
That so much lies ahead for life, for man,
For us; why not for men of the savannah?
Must they be merely set aside for nature?

It seems they must; for here we all love nature,
In Africa at least. "Let kaffir die"
Could be the motto of those green savannah
Groups that strive to save that precious plain
And never give a single thought to man.
Are men somehow less valuable than beasts?

If one loves humans, how can one love beasts?
To survive, a man must conquer nature –
The only other choice, enslave a man
And live a parasite (of course he'll die
But there are others) – this at least is plain.
So, should you ever visit the savannah,

Do ask to see the beasts, to see them die
In glorious nature, death upon the plain:
The bones of man upon the vast savannah.

# Lorelei's Song

If there's reason, I can't recall it,
Why I feel sick and tense.
A fable demands I tell it,
An old tale without sense.

The heavens are cool and dark now,
And quiet flows the Rhine;
The peak of the Rock is a spark now
Of summer eveningshine.

In glory amid the last light
There sits a maid most fair:
Her garment and jewels shine bright
As she combs her golden hair

With a golden comb; and she's singing
The most marvellous song to me.
Even piercing my drums could not bring
Escape from that melody.

In my skiff I am a captive
Of each melodious note,
Caring nothing for the rapids
That wait to sink my boat.

The waves will be devouring,
Too soon, both skiff and I;
And I will die still hearing
The song of Lorelei.

*by Heinrich Heine*
*translated by George J. Dance*

# Index of first lines

www.ingramcontent.com/pod-product-compliance
Lightning Source LLC
Chambersburg PA
CBHW031216090426
42736CB00009B/938